Nursery Rhyme Rally

Jack and Jill went up the hill
to fetch a pail of water.
Jack fell down and broke his crown,
and Jill came tumbling after.

Oh—
A B C D E F G
H I J K L M
N O P Q
R S T U
V W X Y Z!

3

Little Miss Muffet sat on her tuffet
eating her curds and whey.
Along came a spider and sat down beside her
and frightened Miss Muffet away.

4

Oh—
A B C D E F G
H I J K L M
N O P Q
R S T U
V W X Y Z!

Little Boy Blue come blow your horn.
The sheep's in the meadow, the cow's in the corn.
Where is the boy who looks after the sheep?
He's under the haystack fast asleep.

Oh—
A B C D E F G
H I J K L M
N O P Q
R S T U
V W X Y Z!

7

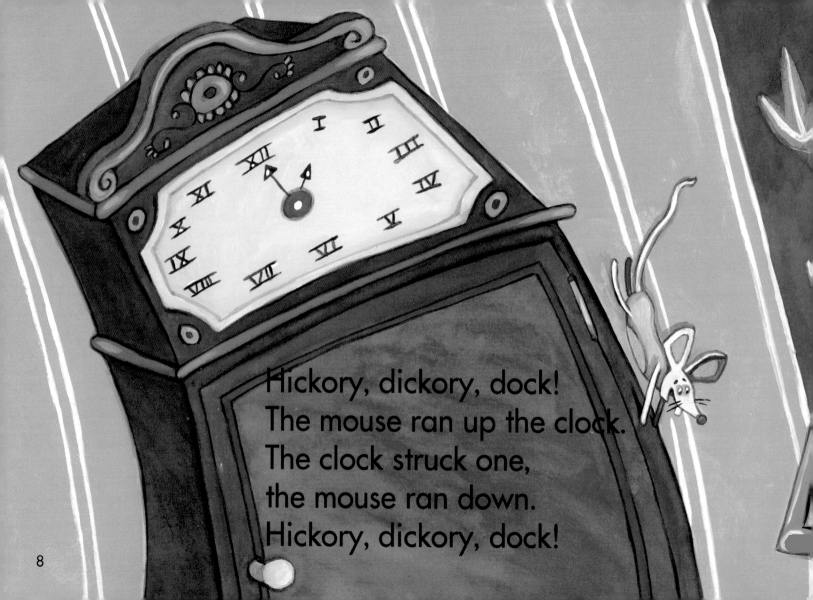

Hickory, dickory, dock!
The mouse ran up the clock.
The clock struck one,
the mouse ran down.
Hickory, dickory, dock!

Mary, Mary, quite contrary,
how does your garden grow?
With silver bells and cockle shells
and pretty maids all in a row.

Oh—
A B C D E F G
H I J K L M
N O P Q
R S T U
V W X Y Z!

Old Mother Hubbard
went to her cupboard
to get her poor dog a bone.
But when she got there
the cupboard was bare
and so that's THE END!

12